The New-Era Entrepreneurial Leader

The Thoughts and Philosophies of One of Asia's Best, Brightest and Promising CEOs

Tomoaki Ota

authorHOUSE®

AuthorHouse™
1663 Liberty Drive
Bloomington, IN 47403
www.authorhouse.com
Phone: 1 (800) 839-8640

Art Credit: Eriko Yamamoto, Enjin Corporation

Published by AuthorHouse 06/23/2016

ISBN: 978-1-5246-1490-4 (sc)
ISBN: 978-1-5246-1491-1 (hc)
ISBN: 978-1-5246-1489-8 (e)

Library of Congress Control Number: 2016909995

Print information available on the last page.

This book is printed on acid-free paper.

Contents

Dedication

I dedicate this book to my two sons, Shin Ota and Jo Ota, in the hopes that some 20 years from now, as they read this book it will help them to think deeply about the decisions they will make in their quests for success and as they encounter challenges which they will inevitably be forced to face.

Introduction

Because of the unique business philosophy from which we operate, our privately owned chemical company not only survived the crisis of the 2011 Great East Japan Earthquake, we actually grew and prospered. As a result of our successful recovery, I published a book in Japan in which I share the philosophies, strategies and thinking that contributed to our recovery and continued growth. In this book I have addressed the growing business challenges in Japan. In doing so, I realize that many of the challenges that Japanese small and mid-sized businesses face are quite similar to those facing small to mid-sized American businesses.

Although I am a Japanese–born businessman, I have been educated in the United States. I have an MBA from Southern Methodist University (SMU) in Dallas, Texas and am a member of the Cox School of Business Alumni Association Board at SMU. Since 2001, I have been president of Johoku Chemical Co., Ltd., a position I assumed at age 36 following the sudden death of my father. It is my connection with America that has prompted me to share with American business leaders many of the same philosophies and thinking published in my Japanese book. The reality is, we are all faced with many of the same global challenges.

Many business leaders are drawn to how-to books written by consultants. These approaches may be useful but in contrast, in this book I share the realities of a company president—not founder—who had to overcome the upheaval of the bursting IT bubble economy, the Lehman Brothers' collapse and the Great East Japan Earthquake and tsunami, all of which happened immediately after assuming my leadership role. When you're facing unanticipated trouble such as this I don't think you can follow a how-to manual. You have to rely on your basic beliefs, principles and philosophies. Throughout this book that is what I will share with you. I will not only touch on concepts but also on technical aspects in various business situations.

Much like in America, where small business is the engine that drives the overall economy, ninety-nine percent of Japanese companies are small to mid-sized and small to mid-sized manufacturing companies largely make up the nation's GDP. Additionally, the technological strength of the manufacturing companies is significant to national policy and as the economy matures, the significance of the service industry increases. However Japan's economy can never exist with its service industry alone. Japan's GDP exceeds 500 trillion yen; it's population exceeds 100 million. Japan is too big to be comparable to countries with financial and service industries such as Hong Kong, Singapore and Luxembourg. Therefore, the manufacturing industry is vital to Japan's economy. But the reality is Japanese manufacturing companies face many challenges due to the changing world—a changing world that also impacts the future of American companies. And while my experience comes from the manufacturing industry specializing in chemical products, and the environment I describe may be different from your industry, it is my desire to provide useful information that all small to mid-sized business leaders will find helpful as we all face the common challenges of economic uncertainty, globalization, a declining birth rate and the retirement of baby boomers, and successfully integrating into business a new Millennial generation of leaders.

As I am somewhat non-traditional in my thinking you will find the format of this book non-traditional also. Rather than chapters filled with laborious explanations of specific procedures or case study examples I have instead merely shared a collection of my thoughts and

philosophies presented in varying sized chapters—
some very small—yet all which I value important
enough to share.

楽しむ (Tanoshimu) That's Japanese for...Enjoy!

Acknowledgments

No one accomplishes success alone. There are individuals and entities that collectively contribute to one's personal gifts and talents. So is the case with my own career so I would like to acknowledge the following for the important roles they have played in my having been blessed to enjoy a wonderful life and operate a successful, profitable business—one which has allowed me to share my philosophies and thoughts in a book like this.

First of all I am thankful for the superb education I received from the Cox School of Business at Southern Methodist University in Dallas, Texas. This education enabled me to broaden my view of achieving in international business.

I thank Chris Bradshaw, my former classmate and the Outreach and Recruitment Director with Goldman Sachs *10,000 Small Businesses* at Dallas County Community College District. She has introduced me to a great network of people in the Dallas area.

I also thank Mr. Satoru Ando, president and CEO of Gephyro Consulting, LLC for helping me to be involved with business activities in Dallas, and Wen Shen in Shanghai.

Thanks also go the Kevin Walker in Dallas and Fabio Okamoto in Sao Paulo, Brazil who have both inspired me in many aspects of my life.

I particularly want to give special thanks to my wife, Mieko Ota, for her faithful and constant support of me.

Finally, I thank you for purchasing this book and I hope that you will find my thoughts and philosophies to be of help to you as you endeavor to enrich your own life and professional path to success.

CHAPTER 1

Break Out of Your Shell— Depart From the Past

On New Year's Day 2001 my father died suddenly. I had joined the chemical company he founded in 1957 just one year before. Although I had earned a Masters in Business Education (MBA) from a graduate school in the U.S. and had worked for major companies in both the U.S. and Japan, I certainly didn't have firsthand knowledge of business management. The different managerial theories I learned through the MBA program and my early business experience were surely helpful, but it is impossible to truly master business management simply from textbooks. So because of my youth and lack of experience, I ended up facing a variety of difficulties soon after assuming the position of president.

It may sound a little argumentative, but in the process of tackling my newfound difficulties and problems, I came to the conclusion that "self-denial" was the solution to many of the issues. The "self" is established over years while experiencing various biases. It is like the self is gathering good and bad moss throughout daily life. This is not a problem if the self gathers only good moss, but there is always an element of biased moss that clouds the eye. Those are subjective views filled with bias, meaningless comparison and jealousy towards others. It is the biased boss that becomes a great problem for business leaders.

In Japan, this biased thinking begins early with the childhood education system. Japan's future is not bright if this problem remains unsolved. Generally speaking, the Japanese education system adopts a relative evaluation process based on points. In this system, students constantly feel pressured to prove how good they are compared to other students and are evaluated by test scores, performance records and which schools they advance to. Unconsciously, and gradually, students begin to focus on comparing themselves with others, setting standards not based on themselves but upon others. In the U.S. it becomes very similar to Asia from the perspective that parents urge their kids to score very high with standardized tests such as SAT and ACT. GPAs are such a great measurement to enter colleges that I hear complaints from teachers that parents often become monster parents. When such an environment exists, students become afraid to disclose their own weaknesses to others.

This fear of divulging weaknesses continues well after the students enter the workplace. It becomes important for them to prove how they can perform better than others. In order to prove this they choose to work longer hours, yet in doing so, get in each other's way. To compete in such a rat race one needs to gain knowledge and skills but a judgmental standard should be based on the individuals themselves rather than one based on the people around them. But in reality, both in school and the corporate system, people are judged based on whether they are superior to others. This system prepares individuals to wear psychological shields to protect themselves which results in individuals only communicating with others through these shields. To put it simply, people act like they get along with each other on the surface but actually they constantly compare themselves with others thus they become annoyed by the small or big differences in others.

Successful business leaders should behave in a completely opposite way. A leader should not focus on him or her self. It is important for a leader to forget self; even deny self. Once an individual denies self he/she can remove the aforementioned biased moss and filter through psychological shields. Just like the proverb states: "The scales fall from one's eye's." By denying self, one can be awakened to the truth.

Soto School Philosophy

Co-founder of Apple, Inc., Steve Jobs, embraced the philosophy of the Soto School which was founded in the 13ᵗʰ century by Dogen Zenji, a Japanese Zen giant. Yakumu Tazato, a scholar of Dogen, called this moment of being awaked by the truth, "absolute knowledge." As an example, carrier pigeons do not use a compass or map to get to destinations. They use absolute knowledge to get there. Salmon also use absolute knowledge to find their way home to lay eggs in their natural stream.

We are all blessed to naturally have this absolute knowledge. People who have this absolute knowledge can tell the difference between counterfeit paintings and real paintings. Steve Jobs, who changed the world, might have realized this simple truth preached by Dogen.

Unfortunately, we suppress our absolute knowledge with our ego.

In "Genjokoan, Actualizing the Fundamental Point" of Schobogenzo, "Treasuring of the True Dharma Eye," Dogen stated the following:

"To study the way is to study self"

"To study the self is to forget the self"

"To forget the self is to be enlightened by all things"

Here, I interpret these statements not from a religious perspective but from a philosophical perspective:

1. To get wisdom, one needs to find the real self = absolute knowledge.
2. To gain absolute knowledge, one should break one's own shell, reject his/her own prejudice in the past, and reset the self.
3. If one can gain absolute knowledge, one will have a natural instinct to handle situations.

People associate Buddhism with a state of perfect selflessness. However, philosopher Dogen preached that it is important to first reach for "self-fulfillment" and then move to "self-transcendence." This is an innovative approach addressed in the 13th century. This idea is similar to that of 20th century American psychologist Abraham Maslow.

I questioned why it is so important to deny the self and why philosophers have been so focused on self-denial in the past. I found my answer to these questions to be quite simple: That is just how it is. Mother nature designed us to force ourselves to break out of our own shells to grow. Fish, animals, human beings—any living objects—experience growing pains in the process of growing. In order for us as business leaders to grow, we must experience the process of growing pains, unlearning and transcending the self.

You might struggle with a feeling of fear of losing the self when you deny yourself. However, you should not be afraid. As "the scales fall from one's eyes" you will be awakened by your real self. The real self includes your strengths, weaknesses and attributes. Once you are awakened by your real self you no longer need to prove how great you are to others. Casually speaking, you realize your limit and your limit is obvious to others—no need to hide it anymore.

When a business leader behaves as if he is better than his employees, no matter how he tries for his best self-fulfillment, it will not benefit the company. Leaders must have employees who possess better skills and knowledge on sales, technology, production, accounting and human resources. He must delegate tasks and expect good results from them. That way the employees will find their own lives worth living through their jobs. This is called empowerment. As a business leader, which would you prefer? You are an enabler but you are tried of working hard with your employees all day and your company is performing badly. Or, your employees fill in the gaps for the parts that you are less capable of, they respect the other employees' autonomy, manage the lower-level employees well and your company performs well.

When I became a business owner in January 2001 after the sudden death of my father, I was very anxious. I believe my employees were also anxious. However, I came out of my shell and overcame the September 11 attacks (which happened soon after assuming the position), the Dot-com Bubble burst, the Lehman Brothers' collapse and the Great East Japan Earthquake as well as the Fukushima nuclear disaster (our plant is located in Iwaki City, Fukushima Prefecture).

I do not claim that my self-fulfillment and ego led to my success in overcoming these crises. I believe that the keys to success are simple: Know your limits, trust your employees, delegate tasks and gain the trust and support of your employees. It may take time to gain the trust of your employees but when you do, together you will be more able to overcome the variety of challenges you are likely to encounter in an ever-changing environment.

My company has had to overcome numerous difficulties since I took over in 2001 yet because of this philosophy I am proud to note that as of the spring of 2016, the company is maintaining a record of the highest sales and profit for six consecutive years. And while I expect that we will be faced with more challenges in the future, I am confident that as a business leader I will stay open-minded and continue to overcome them.

*Dogen: A Japanese Buddhist priest in the Kamakura Period (1185-1333). Founder of the Soto School of Zen in Japan. Known as "Dogen Zenji." Dogen promoted the meditation practice of Zazen. His most famous work, the collection of essays called the Shobogenzo, was studied by many Western philosophers, including Martin Heidegger and Tetsuro Watsuji.

Abraham Maslow: An American psychologist best known for creating Maslow's hierarchy of needs. Maslow hypothesized that humans constantly evolve toward self-actualization, under the theory of five stages of growth. His hierarchy of needs is often portrayed in the shape of a pyramid with the largest, most fundamental levels of needs at the bottom, which is physiological, and then safety, belongingness/love, esteem and self-actualization at the very top. It is believed that only a few percent of people can achieve self-actualization to become self-transcendence. This theory has a common ground with that of Dogen.

CHAPTER 2

Thoughts for Second Generation or Successor

Speaking from personal experience, I think that the second generation or successor of a business will learn the most about being a business leader from outside of his/her company. It is best to gain experiences from major companies because major companies have structured training systems. Successors should start from the bottom of the organization to gain various, and at times, bitter, experiences. This exposes one to the realities of business.

Major Japanese companies are quite strict to newcomers. They are trained to maintain good attitudes and to use proper language in business settings. Honestly, I encountered many unpleasant experience in the first company for which I worked. But now as I look back, I'm glad I had those experiences. I learned first-hand the way employees at the bottom of the organization feel.

Business partners also tend to treat newcomers very strictly because newcomers are simply not yet productive. If newcomers are not productive they are not yet valuable to customers, senior employees or coworkers. They may encounter unusually nice customers once in a while who may be understanding of their newness, but overall the world is severe and cold. Successors need to learn that.

Once a successor becomes a leader they need to stay sensitive to how employees at the bottom of the organization feel, to what kind of environment they are in. Such sensitivities are easy to relate to if an individual has had a difficult time in his/her own early employment experience.

The worse scenario is when a successor joins a family company environment and has great potential but is spoiled because of being a member of the family. Clearly sons and daughters of company owners are favorably treated but I do not believe that company owners should allow their successors to work in their company without having them first gain experiences outside the family owned company.

I realize that there are companies in which family successor members successfully manage the business. However, overall, I personally do not think this approach is a good idea.

Family Business Stock

Although there is benefit to share stocks among family members when several family members are in control of the company's management, many issues arise. I think that a family business needs to be managed by one family member, not by multiple members.

Having two captains on a ship will cause confusion. I think that a company is more disciplined when a president is chosen from the family and no other family members or relatives are employed in the company. Even when only one family member is in charge, problems can also exist when additional family members are involved just as employees.

An American consultant shared with me an example of a family-owned printing business in which one family member was in charge yet several family members were involved as employees. While one family member was president, the other family members held positions in which non-family individuals were their supervisors. However, because the family members saw themselves as "owners" of the business they refused to view themselves as "employees". Thus they failed to respect lines of authority, going to the president with issues instead of going directly to their immediate supervisors. This not only created resentment from the firm's non-family employees, it also created considerable dysfunction in the overall operation. Additionally, because the president was reluctant to reprimand his family members, he spent an inordinate amount of time dealing with issues that should have been handled by their supervisors. This distraction took time away from focusing on the core issues that needed a leader's attention for productive operating and growth.

I realize that there are family businesses that employ members of their own family and operate successfully. However, the truth is that all too often too many of these businesses face family disputes. It is therefore best to avoid this from the beginning by limiting family involvement.

CHAPTER 3

Do Not Compare Yourself to the Founder or Predecessors

The topic of how to relate to a company founder or its predecessors is a difficult one. Second generations or inheritors are more or less conscious of achievements of their predecessors and in most cases, feel their predecessors are greater and that the founder is the greatest.

In order to be acknowledged, inheritors often tend to take various actions such as overextending themselves and acting by reason. But employees will not be fooled by such acts of inheritors. Especially when the inheritor is young. Thus it is not easy to gain absolute trust from employees. So—what should they do?

I found that it is best not to bluff, rather to be humble. Tell employees that you don't know when you don't. When you can't do something, tell them. Instead, find what you can do and do it step by step.

With this honest approach you will gradually gain trust by taking time to overcome various difficulties. When it is something you are not skilled to do, it is better to leave it to someone else who is.

Often a shortcoming of founders is that they believe they understand everything because they started the company. So, they apply the past methods without knowing what has changed in the external environment. There are numerous examples of where a business worsened because a founder was stubborn. When this kind of stubbornness sets in there is no need to follow the founder blindly.

When leadership changes I am sure the new leader is anxious. But employees are equally as anxious. However, when the new leader struggles but then resolves problems and improves the business employees start to think, "Wow, our president is good." You, as the leader, then feel this positive recognition from your employees. Once you get such recognition, all you have to do is maintain it.

Experience gained in schools and entry-level management build knowledge and talent. That knowledge and talent are described as caliber. Business leaders need more caliber but they must also have a certain amount of magnanimity.

Caliber and Magnanimity

Let me explain the difference between caliber and magnanimity. Akiko Takemura, an expert of I Ching, taught me directly that caliber does not mean the level of one's ability, but the wit and skills that someone has. This knowledge is like computer capacity or technological knowledge.

Magnanimity means a person's capacity to accept others' differences in opinions. It is important for business leaders to have wit, experience and skills, but they also must have a great capacity to accept differences. There is a limit in one person's capacity. People will not follow you if you force an issue with such limited capacity. Should they appear to follow they are likely two-faced.

Business leaders maintain their wit and skills gained from experiences. Depending on the situation they may want to purposefully deny their wit and skills to maximize their employees' abilities.

CHAPTER 4

Don't Learn From Seniors

We live in the era of the post-bubble economy, which is completely different from a time of high-speed economic growth. Baby Boomers created the periods of high-speed economic growth and the bubble economy. But I do not think that experiences gained during the days when the economy expanded year after year would come in handy in the slow-growing deflationary period. Businesses based on the asset bubble, such as investments in land and stocks, have already disappeared, thus we must think of business with a new paradigm. Also, the wave of globalism did not exist back then. Moreover, the speed of information transfer is completely different.

I am not criticizing seniors, but I am making the point that times have changed. So from a productive standpoint, what can we learn from the Baby Boomer generation that can be integrated into addressing the needs of the future?

I do think there are many things we can learn from this generation but what I am trying to convey is that their successful stories and measurements will probably not apply to today's business.

In Japan, it is considered a virtue to respect seniors. Our culture emphasizes the importance of listening blindly to what seniors have to say. But we will lose the essence of current activities if we stick to this culture without noticing the changes in the paradigm.

We have much to learn from history and philosophy and there are reasons why the study of history and philosophy still exist. Trendy ideas often disappear in a few days. So I agree that history and philosophy gives us many hints and solutions to changes but business leaders should not be too easily influenced by others' opinions.

There probably is much to learn from the experience of heroes and their spirit of overcoming adversity. Personally, I have learned a lot from biographies of the Roman Emperor Julius Caesar and Marcus Aurelius as well as from the memoirs by Winston Churchill who helped save the United Kingdom. I admire their strong will.

It is important to honor the teachings of those who have come before us yet is also important to do so with the understanding that some of their teachings might need to be modified to be relevant in today's new paradigm.

Consider Study in Liberal Arts

While society demands further advanced specialization, society is not composed of only specializations. For example, a computer systems engineer is not always suited for managing a computer systems company. Hardware was not the only reason for the success of Apple. It was its innovative design that contributed to its success.

The reason headphones produced by Beats, not by Japanese makers, is sweeping the market is not only because of the company's technology, it is also because of its popular design among young people. Product appeal and innovative technology are no longer enough to attract customers.

There was a time when the technology of Japan-made watches was believed to be the best and Swiss watches were thought to be eliminated from the market. At that time many believed that only Japanese quartz watches would survive in the market. Yet at the present time, the market for mid-to-high grade watches is actually monopolized by Swiss makers. People in the world predominantly choose Swiss watches because of their unique designs.

Specializing alone is not good enough in today's advanced global economy and in business, studying business administration and gaining experience as a management consultant will not make you a business leader. One can learn a technical aspect of business, such as accounting, finance or marketing, but one cannot learn the essence of business from schools, books or theories. In order to become a business leader today one is expected to acquire "true culture" in addition to his/her specialty.

In the U.S. many universities focus on the liberal arts. Many students acquire bachelor degrees in liberal arts and then advance to graduate schools to specialize in specific subjects. Moreover, many students take liberal arts classes even if they advance in universities that offer specialized courses. Many people believe that the study of liberal arts is equal to the study of only humanities courses. This is not true. Liberal arts classes include many science and math classes. In Japan, university students are separated into science majors and humanities majors at an early stage, and they are treated as if they are different races. Leonardo da Vinci excelled in various fields such as art, humanities and science. Liberal arts include all aspects of Western civilization.

We also need to check what exists in Eastern civilizations, but I feel overwhelmed with the abundance of Eastern philosophy and sometimes feel at a loss when I consider where to start.

I recommend finding Eastern philosophy that suits you the best. Personally, I prefer I Ching, the oldest of the Four Books and Five Classics, that existed from the beginning of the Chinese civilization, as well as the philosophy of the Soto school founded by Dogen, whom Apple co-founder Steve Jobs embraced. I smile smugly at the fact that the great innovator of the present age, Steve Jobs, was very much interested in Dogen.

Except for those in the engineering field, many people study law and business. I think that while polishing those specialties, business leaders will absorb ideas from various fields and apply those ideas to their business practices.

Absorbing abundant knowledge will help leaders expand their creativity and flexibility and help them to better meet the needs of today's changing customer demands.

CHAPTER 5

Reality: Family and Self Are More Important Than Company

In Japan, people often talk about management focusing on employees. However, I wonder if employees feel that their companies focus on them. A sweatshop-like work environment has recently been reported in Japan, but I think that is not really the problem. I think the problem is that long-term employees maintain their employment despite their complaints and relationship problems. They are hesitant to speak up because of their longtime employment status.

No matter how much a business owner says to the employees, "Think of the company first," it is themselves and their families that are most important to them. So, if that's true, why do employees also care about their companies? They care about their companies because it provides the employment for them to make a living, not because the companies have a great priority in their lives. Sometimes business owners misunderstand this because they themselves put such a priority on their companies.

It is important for business leaders to keep in mind that a company exists first in an employee's mind to earn one's bread and butter, and simply to perform work that cannot be done alone. One person can do much but it may be inefficient to do it all alone. Novelists and artists and similar professions may probably do all the work required by working alone. However, a business like manufacturing needs people to make things, thus such work cannot be done alone. If you were to suddenly ask someone from accounting to work in production they would likely be unable to do so. Individuals have different talents and skills. Some people are skilled at marketing and sales while the same people may not be as skilled at the work that develops new products. It takes a variety of talents and skills for the entire company to succeed.

Since people must often work together to get the job done, a cooperative attitude, a sense of volunteerism, compromise, self-assertion and self-denial may emerge. Companies are not public service entities, thus they must generate profits. Therefore, employees must contribute to generating profits. I think it is wrong for some employees to claim only their own rights and turn everything into harassment issues (often with no viable grounds). Employees may need to claim their rights in companies if a sweatshop-like environment exists. But otherwise, when employees reflect on themselves and deeply think about what "work" really means to them without bias, I believe that employees will realize what they can bring to their companies and thus act accordingly. The fruit of those acts will then lead to increased sales and profits, which should eventually return to the employees as benefits.

Business leaders should not treat their employees as if they are personal belongings and employees should view their work as their tools for self-actualization. Then both leaders and employees can deepen their relationships and consequently, this trusting relationship will help to contribute to resolving many of the recent mental health issues and harassment suits that impact some companies.

On the issues of transfers, while I understand that periodical reassignments may be necessary, there are many cases in major companies where employees are arbitrarily transferred every year with no consideration given to family affairs such as schools and housing. In some cases, employees are transferred alone without their families. There may be a case where this is unavoidable for business reasons, but I don't think employees or their families are happy with such transfers. I see this kind of transfer as being done just to make the point of a company-centered culture. And while I understand that periodical reassignments may be necessary, I don't agree that some companies are taking transfer actions strategically. It seems nonsense to rationalize to employees that the reason for making transfers is because of internal change. Usually it takes five years, if not ten, to master one assignment effectively. Our company never takes such forcible transfer actions. It impacts the employee's family negatively, which eventually impacts the company as well.

I believe maintaining long term employee assignments, while keeping close communications with employees, will best benefit companies and employees and even business partners. A well-known American psychologist, Abraham Maslow, describes human needs as ordered in a hierarchy. Maslow's hierarchy of needs explains the stages of human desires in which the most fundamental basic needs, such as a physiological and safety need must be met before an individual reaches self-actualization (the highest stage). If self-actualization of each employee can be achieved directly or indirectly through employment, the power of an organization will itself become enormous.

CHAPTER 6

Lack of Future Business Leaders a High Risk

Japan today faces a variety of challenges, most significant a declining birth rate. In 2013 the birth rate in Japan reached as low as that of 1885 with just 1.03 million. In 1885 Hirofumi Ito became the prime minister of the country. Japan was a developing country with an unpromising future. As Japan developed, the birth rate drastically increased, reaching its peak of 2.69 million in 1949. After a brief spell of stagnation, the birth rate began to increase during the baby boom generation, ending at 2.09 million in 1973. However since then, the birth rate has been in decline.

A similar situation exists in the U.S. where the birthrate dropped to a historic low in 2013, disappointing those who had been waiting for a strong rebound. From 2012 to 2013 the number of births fell by 20,000.

When the population increases in developing countries every family member counts as laborers when it comes to the primary industry. The more the society grows economically, the more the cost of living and education for children increases. But Japan has now reached a point where having many children in a household causes more financial burdens to families.

A decrease in population naturally reduces consumer demand unless consumers are encouraged to spend extravagantly as they did during the bubble economy period. With an enactment of the Recycling Law and other spending disciplines, on top of an increase in sales tax, the Japanese economy is experiencing a downturn in consumption. No matter how hard the Bank of Japan strengthens its monetary easing policy, people are not tempted to spend more; furthermore, many people are concerned with the nation's social welfare system. Again, similar impact is being seen in the U. S. economy.

The problem in Japan is not just the decline in population or consumption. "A quality population" appears to be the problem. I do not want to criticize the younger generation by saying, "Kids nowadays...." however, it is evident that how the younger people play is completely different from how the middle-aged and older people used to play in their childhoods. Today's children in Japan do not play outside due to safety concerns; rather they mainly play video games inside. I don't want to criticize video games as they may contribute to improving the processing power of computers, but the problem is how much time children spend on playing video games. While it depends on individual families, I wonder if overall children don't play at least a half-hour to a few hours each day. When you multiply those hours by 365 days, that's significant; it wastes precious childhood time when many opportunities exist to learn. With the popularity of video games and social networking, these technological distractions are a factor that impacts not just the Japanese culture but many other cultures as well.

Many aspects of our lifestyles have become more convenient via technology. An automated bathtub system is a good example. With the push of a button not only can water be set by a timer to be heated, but also the water quality and temperature can also be set. Back in the old days people used firewood. In Japan, many people also experienced a balanced-flue gas water heater for their bathtubs. The process went like this: You turn on the water. After a while you go back to check to see if the water quantity is appropriate and stop the water. Sometimes you make a mistake by letting the water run too long. You heat the water, checking to see if the fire is on or if the temperature is warm enough, then you decide whether the water needs to be heated a little longer. This is just one example of the fact that we used to have many ways in our lifestyles that required us to think and adjust as things move forward. Today it seems like everything only depends on pushing a button—programming television shows, using most home appliances, using the Internet and even reserving a taxi.

I fear that people who grow up in this one-push-of-a-button society have been losing their sense of intuition, which is important for all humans to possess. Humans naturally have a wonderful power called "Absolute Knowledge." As we continue to face an aging population, people who no longer possess such a power will be those who enter the workplace of the future.

Frankly speaking, I wonder if this poor quality of workers, coupled with the decreasing population, will be able to support our country's economy and create business leaders. Some may disagree, but I think that the baby boom generation and older generations are responsible for the problems that our country will face in the future. They are responsible because they are the ones who have formed the current social structure. Handing down the problems to the next generation and saying, "Good Luck," after their retirement will not work. It will be irresponsible of them to hand down problems to the next generation. Leaders in government, business and education seem hesitant to tackle the population problem. They are not able to come up with drastic resolve measures. Rather they issue huge sums in deficit-covering government bonds and procrastinate solving problems. In Japan, for example, debt is twice as much as its GDP (Gross Domestic Product) while in the U. S. debt maintains its debt as equal to its GDP. In short, there are an increasing number of people in the younger generation who lack adequate problem-solving skills.

A decline in the birth rate, an increase in the aging population and a change in the temperament of the younger generation will turn into major problems in the future. Under such circumstances, the lack of successors for small and mid-sized businesses, which support Japan and U.S. economies, will present a huge obstacle.

Having taken over the business after the sudden death of my father, I am deeply concerned if the younger generation in Japan can run businesses in the midst of turbulent times. That is why in this book I share my 15 years of experience and struggles as a young business leader, especially with the younger and future business leaders of Japan. I hope that sharing my experiences will provide some positive guidance to future business leaders.

CHAPTER 7

Media Reports Shouldn't Influence Uncertainty

What is required for business leaders but not for employees is to stay acutely aware of the sense of uncertainty about the future. It is dangerous for leaders to be overly influenced by media reports. For example, we read that the Lehman Brothers' collapse was a crisis occurring once in 100 years. Yet who could have predicted how long that unprecedented crisis would last? Many companies became extremely pessimistic and laid off numbers of employees. Then when the economy recovered many companies could not manufacture due to lack of employees. Consequently several lost market share and business deals and eventually withdrew from the market.

I recommended that business leaders simply do not depend on information from the media, such as newspapers and news reports. Instead, I believe leaders should carefully follow and analyze economic daily macro data themselves rather than relying on analysis charts created by staff or consultants. By dealing with data yourself, you are able to see things from your own perspectives and get a stronger sense of what is really happening.

The good news is that all necessary data can be easily obtained from the Internet. I can only assume that readers of this book are comfortable using the Internet and spreadsheets. By creating and analyzing your own spreadsheets, you will intuitively grasp changes in the economy.

Depending solely on others and asking others how the situation is going to change will not help you predict upcoming changes.

In Japan many business leaders rely on "Tankan," issued by the Bank of Japan. It is one of the key financial measures in Japan and has considerable influence in stock prices and the currency rate. Tankan is released as an index for economic trends. This indicator is similar to America's Institute of Supply Management (ISM) manufacturing index, which tracks the amount of manufacturing activity that occurred in the previous month. In the U. S. this is considered a very important and trusted economic measure. If the index has a value below 50 because of decreased activity, the index tends to indicate an economic recession—particularly if the trend continues over several months. When the index has a value above 50 it likely indicates a time of economic growth.

Personally, while Tankan and ISM provide important numbers, I don't believe these numbers can be used to predict long-term analysis. Personally finding, gathering and manipulating data myself by studying macroeconomics has been more useful to me.

In order to get an idea of future changes, I personally collect, process and analyze data from the "Indices of Industrial Production (IIP), "Indices of Inventory Ration," "Purchasing Managers Index," and "The Number of Manufacturing Workers." Following is information on each.

The Indices of Inventory Ratio Reflects to the Economy

The inventory ratio index is formulated by dividing the inventory index by the shipment index. In simple terms when inventory increases, the inventory ratio index increases. When the shipment index increases, the inventory ratio index decreases. During the Lehman Brothers' collapse the inventory ratio index rapidly increased. The sudden rise was because no sales were made and business inventories increased more than usual. Our company's sales were down then, consistent with the index. As long as the ratio index does not make a sudden rise, the economy is good and business is as usual. Even if the media reports are pessimistic and the Bank of Japan's "Tankan" indicates low or high numbers, there is no need to panic.

China and the Purchasing Managers Index (PMI) for the Manufacturing Industry

China is our very important partner and competitor. China's economic trend greatly influences our country's economy. However it is not possible to obtain much historic economic data for China. Therefore, the Purchasing Managers Index (PMI) is a very effective tool to analyze the business trends. The PMI for the manufacturing industry goes up when Chinese companies believe the economy is good and it goes down when they foresee the economy is bad. Generally speaking, major manufacturing companies believe that the economy is good when the index is higher than 50 and the economy is bad when it is lower than 50.

I mentioned earlier that "Tankan" is of no use because it is vague. However, the ambiguous figure like PMI helps visualize the trend of a big country like China and this is the only tool we can use.

The Number of Manufacturing Industry Workers

It is important to closely monitor changes in the number of manufacturing industry workers in the long term. Both in the U.S. and Japan, we naturally emphasize the unemployment rate to map out financial policies. Since the unemployment rate applies to all industries it does not show the actual situation specific to the manufacturing industry. Therefore I determined that the trend in the number of manufacturing industry workers reflected the actual condition in the industry. I then compared the trend in the number of manufacturing industry workers in the U.S and Japan, extracting data since 1950 from the U.S. Department of Labor and the Statistics Bureau of the Ministry of Internal Affairs and Communications in Japan. I was able to obtain this data from the Internet. It turned out to be very interesting:

1. The highest number of workers in the U.S. was 20 million while in Japan it was 17 million. If we consider the U.S. population is two to three times greater than Japan's population, these numbers tell us that Japan had a large number of manufacturing workers in the past. This tells us that Japan is a country of strong craftsmanship.

2. The U.S. reached its peak number of manufacturing workers in the 1970's. The numbers declined with the economic decline and the transition into service-related industry.

3. Japan reached its peak numbers of manufacturing workers during the bubble economy. Since then

the numbers have decreased from 17 million to the present number of 10 million.

4. Due to the Fed's easing after the Lehman Brothers' collapse, the number of manufacturing industry workers in the U.S. hit bottom. That is now slowly recovering.

Globalization and capitalism giving power to stockholders, led Japan to take shortsighted actions. Despite the fact that Japan used to have a large number of manufacturing industry workers in the past compared to the U.S., over time Japan's shortsighted actions caused a decrease in the number of manufacturing industry employees and an outflow of its technology to foreign countries. The country's attitude during the bubble economy was awful. It was like silently rushing into a war, creating chaotic bubbles and adopting globalization in a self-harmful manner. I do not think that Japan's weakening of the manufacturing industry and the outflow of technology will create long-term benefits or happiness for Japan's people.

Japan was about to establish its own business model when the bubble burst. We did not take any drastic measures to prevent the weakening of the manufacturing industry. I am disappointed with the government and major companies for that lack of intervention.

Small to mid-sized companies somehow need to figure out how to survive under such conditions. There is no textbook answer to that. Instead, we must think of and find an appropriate measure. It won't be easy, but I think we—small to mid-sized companies—must find a way. We should not be influenced by the directions of major companies or by trendy theories. If we do, we will end up failing. We first need to evaluate strengths, weaknesses, opportunities and threats (SWOT analysis) and then execute appropriate measures at the right time.

In our company we took the following measures: a strategic reinforcement of our supplies, going against the belief in Just-in-Time (JIT) manufacturing; maintenance of the Japanese-style lifetime employment system and seniority system; conservative and gradual capital investment; purchase of various options to protect the company from market changes; the building of long-term partnerships with foreign companies rather than costly entry into overseas markets; the abolishment of rigid budgeting; and the abolishment of mid-term plans. We must not only plan, we must execute the plan.

This must be working. As of the end of our fiscal year 2015 our company posted record revenue for the fifth straight year.

CHAPTER 8

It's Not Where You Came From, But Where You Are Heading

I like the movie *Public Enemies*, starring Johnny Depp. The movie is about John Dillinger, a notorious bank robber. During the Great Depression bank robbers got a lot of attention because they attacked banks that had, in some people's opinions, taken advantage of a vulnerable group of people.

In the movie, Dillinger and his girlfriend, who comes from a lower class, are having dinner in a very nice restaurant. Dillinger says to the girlfriend, "Those fellows are all worried about where they come from. They proudly talk about their social class and what they have done in the past. What is the most important is not who you are or where you come from but what you are going to do from now on."

People who inherit businesses often come from privileged families and sometimes they try to use the influence of their ancestry to impress others. However, things like ancestry are not important to employees. To them, it is irrelevant if you are the son or daughter of the founder. What is important is just like Dillinger said, it is what you will do in the future.

In the end, we are all humans. Once people start to think that relations within the family mean privilege, the family business will start to decline. Stock possession is merely important as it relates to the legal aspect of the company. It does not appeal to employees. Only when a family business brings happiness to all of its employees will that business succeed.

Destiny is Not Set

Masahiro Yasuoka, a Japanese scholar of Yangmingism, was a mentor for many politicians during modern times in Japan. Yangmingism is one of the major philosophical schools of Neo-Confucianism, based on the idea of Neo-Confucian philosopher Wang Yangming, who developed as the main intellectual opposition to the Cheng-Zhu school of Neo-Confucianism.

According to Yasuoka, the idea that destiny is already set is not true. Fate, on the other hand, is beyond one's control.

An airplane crash, death from a disease, death by war or earthquake—those are examples of fate and one cannot avoid these scenarios. However, a human has the power to forge his or her destiny, but that may require effort. This is called "Ritsumei."

In short, Destiny = Fate + Ritsumei

I really like this Japanese word. Its translation is:

> To make your life by yourself
>
> To make your life stand by yourself
>
> To build your life by yourself

Our language explains these meanings by only two words: 立命

The first character symbolizes to stand (this looks like the person is standing.

The second character symbolizes life (this looks like a man with a cap praying for his life).

You cannot escape from fate, but, in our lives, we must have "Ritsumei" to forge our destiny while using our full talents. Otherwise, there is no reason to make any effort. Business leaders should make full use of their talents and skills to create the "Ritsumei" of their own companies. In other words, with "Ritsumei" one has the power to forge his own destiny with the exception of fate.

CHAPTER 9

The Application of Contradiction

What I'm about to discuss may sound more philosophical than business oriented. But, bear with me as I have found it to be a very powerful business tool. It's the idea of "self contradiction."

The idea of "self-contradiction" is very important to followers of Hegelianism, the philosophy of the 18th Century German philosopher, G. W. F. Hegel which concludes that "the rational alone is real," therefore all reality is capable of being expressed in rational categories.

The universe contains contradictions, yet develops toward one direction while repeating three dialectical stages of development: a thesis, an antithesis and a synthesis, which reaches sublation (elimination or to negate but preserve a partial element of synthesis). Here, contradictions can be the result of various problems, Mother Nature or setbacks. In short, a thesis given to rise to an antithesis, which contradicts the thesis and the tension between the two is constructively integrated (sublation) and is resolved by means of a synthesis. This is called the dialectic method, which is a very powerful tool in business.

Business leaders face contradictions in organizations and in society. By applying this method, leaders accept opposite opinions rather than linearly pursue sound arguments. Saying, "Listen to what I say," does not help an organization. This idea endorses the way to motivate people who received uniformed educations. Humans and Mother Nature are not linearly formed; they are complicated beings.

I found that the progression of the airplane gave me a good example to apply the dialectic method to business. I enjoy flying, as I like to travel overseas. Looking at an airplane, it's easy to simply wonder how that large lump of iron gets off the ground. As everyone knows, a genius like Galileo or Leonardo da Vinci could not have invented an airplane overnight. It had to be a progression. I realized that it had to begin with paper planes, then moved to gliders and later engines with propellers were added, which eventually were replaced with jet-engines. Suddenly we had a jet-engine airplane made of a mass of metal with engines and computers and it flies. This contradiction, that a lump of iron could fly, technically reached to a synthesis only after inventors applied the dialectic method and step-by-step made small progress through a trial and error process that went on for many years. I imagine that the inventors experienced countless failures and sacrifices to get there. Similarly, I realized that technology, companies and personalities also do not get better overnight. They evolve and grow over years while experiencing contradictions and setbacks.

It is actually not hard to apply this dialectic method to business. For example, it is hard to reach an agreement in a meeting but by taking time to constructively discuss an agenda, participants can reach a degree of consensus. This is not always a compromise.

In the development of the dialectic method there is a theory of plasticity. Plastic becomes flexible with heat, which makes it possible to be processed. However, depending on how you use it, plastic can become a destructive force, like a bomb, or a good force like a usable product. Dr. Catherine Malabou, a modern French philosopher, calls for a theory of plasticity in the dialectic method. She believes that after a certain period of time, reforms and innovative ideas may arise. In my previous example of the airplane, these reforms and innovative ideas led to propellers, jet engines and eventually computers. Today, the Internet creates many similar innovative ideas.

In developing the dialectic method, people create small innovations. This is called the synergy effect.

Our company has maximized the synergy effect by evolving certain products for new uses, such as parts for automobiles, printing materials, medical products, plastics and electronics. This evolution has created additional products, thus additional profits.

The dialectic method is a little bit reserved, but once you get the key points it becomes a powerful tool for business. If you're not particularly interested in philosophy and decide to consider studying the German philosophy, you will most likely be buried under an enormous amount of theories. But I suggest that you can still benefit from this if you simply learn the main points and apply them with experience. Then perhaps you too will find new ways to expand your products, services and profits.

CHAPTER 10

Wars Help Demonstrate The Difference Between Strategy and Tactics

Japanese people like to rush blindly into decision, consequently fall into the never-say-die spirit. As a result, when a person is a cog in a wheel of an organization they often do not understand the difference between strategy and tactics. I used to be one of those people.

Strategy applies at a high level; it implies the significance of the existence and the purpose of the company. Tactics implies plans to accomplish the strategy. Therefore, there is a whole difference between strategic thinking and tactical thinking. It is meaningless to win in tactics if you lose in strategies.

It is easy to criticize tactics after the fact. Take the Pacific War as an example. The Japanese Imperial Navy made a great success on Pearl Harbor by making the first-ever move on the enemy territory with a large-scale use of aircraft carriers. Strategically this was a huge failure because this attack made the U.S. serious about the war against Japan and eventually led to Hitler's declaration of war against the U.S. Just as politicians are responsible for strategically leading the country in the right direction so are business leaders responsible for strategically leading their companies in the right direction.

Germany, exulted in its quick success over France, thus started the battle on the Eastern Front against the Soviet Union. Although the war against France was tactically successful, the battle on the Eastern Front was a big failure because the invasion triggered the support of the U.S. for the Soviet Union.

In corporate settings, let's say that a company makes a huge business investment in response to interim business expansion. This may be tactically successful, resulting in business expansion but can be a strategic failure when the company faces a period of decline in demand. A case in point is Sharp Corporation. This company, with its world-class technology, is facing difficulty in its operations after it made an excessive investment and aggressive business plan for a solar battery. With the solar battery industry having structural problems throughout the world, it has become more expensive than other electrical systems; so expensive it could not even be sustained by government subsidy. For example a German company that once prospered went bankrupt after the government stopped its subsidy. Thus, Sharp's solar battery production has not produced positive results.

Strategy has a broad definition. It has become popular for many companies to set up mission statements. However, many mission statements, including those of many U.S. companies, are unclear and senseless. "Contributing to society," "Environmentally friendly," or "Pursue mutual coexistence"—these are expected things and should not even have to be stated in mission statements. Moreover, such statements as "Decouple sales," or "Become the top player in the industry," only reflect an owner's ambitions and show no concern with the interests of their employees or their customers.

Our company's mission statement is very tangible:

"Our company maintains sustainable domestic growth by developing and selling highly value-added chemical products. Our company targets a two-percent sales increase every year and maintains a ten-percent recurring profit margin."

Japanese companies are good at planning tactics. A group of experts can create a strategy that stands out and they can execute it and business owners assume the leadership of managing this group of "super-generalists." Logistics are also important. Logistics in a corporate setting means not only distribution but also includes finance management. The Japanese Imperial Army made light of military logistics. Consequently, the U. S. submarines destroyed the oil conveyance to Southeast Asia.

Since the Roman Empire, Western countries have had greater logistic skills and are still superior in this field. Businesses can benefit from doing the same.

Be Timid, Be Cautious

I also think business leaders should be timid. There are many past cases in which recklessness led to countries falling apart or companies going out of business. An analogy from Japanese culture is that only timid tropical fish survive and grow bigger. Bold tropical fish are eaten before getting big.

It has been said that Konosuke Matsushita, the founder of Panasonic, could not sleep as he worried too much about his company. Even the first German Chancellor, Bismarck, said a timid general is the best because he does not risk his army recklessly.

In Japan, Oda Nobunaga is known as the boldest, yet feudal, warlord. He was bold, but in many cases he also took cautious actions. He spent 17 years overthrowing the most powerful Takeda clan. While Oda displayed a conciliatory attitude with Takeda Shingen—even having his adopted daughter marry

Takeda's son in 1565—Oda started a battle against Takeda in 1572.

In 1573 Takeda died. Oda then defeated Takeda Katsuyori, his son-in-law, in the Battle of Nagashino in 1575 and the Takeda Clan fell in Nagashima.

Like Oda, by having a timid attitude, business leaders can evaluate countermeasures and stimulate plans to handle various risks.

CHAPTER 11

The Importance of Positive and Negative

For several years I have been attending a study group for I Ching, the oldest of the Four Books and Five Classics. Four Books are Chinese classic texts that illustrate the core value and belief systems in Confucianism. The Five Classics are five pre-Quin Chinese books that constitute part of the traditional Confucian canon.

According to I Ching, there are "yin" and "yang" in things. "Yin" is not necessarily bad and "yang" is not necessarily good. For example, "yang" is the daytime and "yin" is the nighttime. No living things can survive without both day and night.

In the Western business world, being positive is seen as good. An annual ten percent increase in sales, high profits, pay increases, an expansion of market share—are all things that are seen as positive.

However, there is always a negative behind a positive. There is a "yin" behind a "yang." This is the natural order of things. There is no way for anyone to think positively all the time.

In the business community no one is conscious of "yin;" probably because we are influenced by capitalism and expansionism. When governments continue to borrow they often default. In the case of a business, when this happens the business goes bankrupt. Interest rates should be raised to prevent the burst of a bubble. But the reverse action is taken at present. An increase in interest rates in this instance implies the "yin." Of course extreme "yin" is not good, but a gentle use of "yin" *is* good. The reality is when the government keeps encouraging expansion, consequently the bubble bursts and the country's economy and its people end up being impacted by the damage.

Business leaders need to acknowledge such situations objectively and immediately use "yin" when they notice overheated situations. If you realize you have worked too much, you take a break. If plant operations go too far, maintenance needs to be done. So, there are many occasions where "yin" can be used. Unfortunately, many companies do not realize when to use "yin." As a result many business leaders and their employees eventually get worked up and crash. For example, a business that opens up new stores too fast may fall into an unprofitable state after reaching a certain number of stores.

Despite the fact that the concept of "yin" and "yang" has existed in Japan in the form of the Chinese classics for a long time, it is not effectively utilized in businesses. Often it is misunderstood and people think than this concept means to stay in the middle between "yin" and "yang." What needs to be noted is that the concept of "yin" and "yang" does not mean one has to stay in the middle between "yin" and "yang." One merely needs to be aware of the concept and use it accordingly.

The Power of Concentration is Also Important

Business leaders must also show the power of concentration. As a company grows, business fields expand and it becomes impossible to cover it all. Leaders need to focus on handling each business aspect one-by-one. The idea of "here-and-now" exists globally. In this era of the Internet people think multitasking is a talent. But it is not the case for business leaders. *Power of Now: A Guide to Spiritual Enlightenment* by Eckhart Tolle has been a best seller in Western countries for several years. The book stresses the importance of living in the present moment.

Likewise, Zen also stresses to focus on the "here-and-now." "Shoko Kyakka" is a Japanese term that means, "to look carefully where your own footsteps fall." And the term "Zengo Saidan" means, "not to be influenced by others." So as mentioned earlier, to maximize the power of concentration one must manage one's own time and stretch every nerve to handle an issue. The tip of the arrow is effective only when it is sharp.

Just like a sniper, business leaders are expected to focus step-by-step to effectively solve problems.

Leaders Need Not Distinguish Between Private and Business Matters

I clearly remember a time when I ran into an executive of a publicly listed company in central Ginza. Ginza is a popular upscale shopping area of Tokyo and is known for attracting visitors from around the globe.

The first thing this executive asked me was if I was there privately or for business. I remember I was disappointed to be asked that question. Probably, in his mind, there was a clear distinction between private and business matters when one spends time in an area like Ginza. And, depending upon which

I responded, his remarks and actions may change. I do understand since I realize that the conduct of executives of well-known companies like his are often reported on by the media.

Business leaders in small to mid-sized companies should have no distinction between what they do in their private lives versus their official lives. It is not a mixture of official or private matters but the co-existence of these two. My employees may think that I am not working when I'm in a place like Ginza, but often I am thinking about business when I'm not working. The fact is, I often think more about business outside the company than when I am in the company. Therefore, there is no distinction for me between my private and business lives. This does not mean that I use the company's property in private activities but in my thought process, there is no distinction between one's private and business lives. The reality is, business owners of small to mid-sized companies cannot escape from managing the business. They may take a break, but they cannot ever get away from their ultimate responsibility.

Hired executives eventually retire. Politicians often say that they will resign to take responsibility for some action. But in my opinion, resigning is not taking responsibility. How people take responsibility nowadays is often a double standard as they focus on what is most convenient for them. As the owner of a small to mid-sized business taking responsibility is always a priority of one's mind regardless of whether you are on private or business time.

CHAPTER 12

What's the Point?

Japanese people, in general, are good at circular reasoning. In circular reasoning people often start a conversation with an irrelevant topic and develop the conversation to a point at the end. This approach is the result of the Japanese language itself, which is structured in the form of circular reasoning. This style is not consistent with the Western style of theoretical story composition and development. I personally think that the Japanese language has an outstanding communication technique in this circular style in which points are naturally embedded into the conversation.

However this Japanese style of communication does not work well when communicating with Westerners. Here, communicating in a very direct style works better.

I don't want to confuse you, but I find that Westerners also have a gap between real intentions and a public stance. This tendency might be rather stronger than that of the Japanese people. Nevertheless, no one will understand you if you do not speak straight to the point—especially in the business world.

In the U.S. it is common to use a proposal called an executive summary. Statistical and qualitative facts are included in this one-page summary. In some ways proposals created by Japanese business people often contain redundant explanations and too many pages. In this regard, American business people have excellent skills to make a point succinctly and effectively. Thus, I think it may be best to prepare an executive summary and then, if you are presenting to Japanese counterparts, I suggest you adapt the proposal to suit the Japanese way of communication.

In short, the important thing to keep in mind is to always remember what your point is and how your respective audience will best receive it.

Stop Immediately When You Notice Mistakes

I know a business owner who became aware that he had made a mistake but was not willing to switch direction. He ended up worsening the damage. Behavioral economics points out that a business owner will sometimes make a wrong business decision and continue to invest in the business, getting stuck with a cost of the past, even though it is no longer effective. It is a cost that in the past may have been acceptable but once obsolete, that cost should not affect the future.

An example of this mistake would be the hundreds of millions of dollars spent on a development project in the past where the business owner is unable to make a decision to back off from the project when it is no longer viable. When the past development is no longer useful for the future of the business, any continued investment in the development becomes a wasted cost. Business leaders should not be emotionally attached to these kind of past costs.

In my opinion, Japanese people, in general, are not good at recognizing when to stop investing in projects or developments that are no longer viable. In our culture, some business people are too committed to the word "Ganbatte," which means, "to do the best." Although I do not deny the idealism of "Ganbatte," it does not mean anything if all of the best that one continues to do results in a failure.

Western people also seem to be quick to attack but also fast to pull out. They immediately withdraw when they think something will not work.

I believe Japanese small to mid-sized companies should be more aggressive about making strategic withdrawals from certain markets when they show indications of change. It is not a shame to acknowledge a loss and move on to the next situation. To deny this option could be a total loss if lack of courage caused a country, a company or a family to be destroyed. History shows that generals need to be able to decide quickly from the front when it is necessary. That is wise advice for business owners as well.

Don't Risk Want of Courage

People play percentages in this society. There is little difference in this idea between Japan and the U.S. If one accomplishes something noticeable, they might weigh whether he or she may suffer from their decision, be criticized or be sued on unreasonable grounds. The higher one secures a position, the more they may worry or become depressed. However, I would tend to criticize this caution, as it's better to do something than nothing.

In the Analects of Confucius there is a saying: "Knowing what is right and not doing it is a want of courage." This happens when one turns a blind eye to an injustice or to an obligation. When this happens, courage does not exist. I'm not suggesting that one should save the world by sacrificing oneself, however, the fact is that there are so many things we witness and act on with a little bit of courage. Yet often we fail to do so because we believe doing so is not advantageous to us. So, we play the percentages.

No matter how small something might be, by taking little-by-little actions, business leaders will grow personally and this growth will lead to business success in the long run. Such an approach also works in one's personal life. The Hindu scripture *Upanishad* stated that it is important to understand that selfless acts become the strongest arms. This was written in India in ancient times, yet it deeply relates to Indian culture, including Hinduism and Buddhism and the formation of the nation. It is a scripture important to consider as one weighs their future decisions.

CHAPTER 13

The Four "Don'ts" of Success

Don't be suckered into theories. Because Japanese people are such diligent workers this may be a reason why they can easily be sucked into trendy theories. But trendy business terms, much like trendy fashions, can be quickly forgotten with time. It's easy to lose insights if one is too easily influenced by such trends. Japanese people also like to use imported words from Western countries; words like focus, core competencies, compliance, scheme and manifest to name a few. However, these words can often be misinterpreted and their meaning can become vague and/or exaggerated. I think every leader needs to use words from their own cultures to ensure clarity and total understanding.

What one gains too easily can also be lost so easily. Also, a person can master just about anything if they spend time to learn about it. But what one learns overnight by cramming can quickly disappear the very next day. For example, many people have not remembered details of history that they studied in order to pass an entrance exam for college. "Easy come, easy go," as the saying goes. This same idea applies to relationships as well. People keep their friendships with their classmates yet it is not easy to make lifelong friendships in work settings. It's the same for love. Love developed quickly often fails to last long.

One might think of it this way. In the theory of heat transfer, cooking pots made of iron or aluminum get hot quickly, but they cool down quickly too. It takes time to heat up stone pots, but once one is heated it holds the heat. Just like this rule of nature, it takes time to create a quality object or accomplish something important. It took me time to understand this rule because I am impatient and because of my American education, I have been influenced by the fast-paced U. S. society. Yet once I understood and accepted this I realized how much good sense it made.

I also have come to know that throughout our lives we will run into situations where things cannot be explained by reason. I have also learned that knowledge and languages are not the only influences. Zen Buddhism teaches "Furyu Monji," which explains that the essence of things can be expressed neither by words nor by theories. The reality is, some things just are. So, don't be suckered into theories.

Don't diversify business. I believe that small to mid-sized companies with little capital should not diversify their businesses. Make just one mistake and it could be fatal. But a product diversification that creates a synergistic effect within one company can be good. The Lanchester strategy, a war strategy that has been successfully applied in the business context, states, the weak must not spread out its force but focus on one thing to compete.

It is tempting to diversify a business when the economy is good, but, as is said, "Lights are usually followed by shadows." When the economy is good a company should create a solid footing and invest in its areas of specialty. It is important that sometimes business leaders need to have the courage *not* to take any actions.

Don't go for overseas expansion. I am not in favor of overseas expansion for production operations by small to mid-sized manufacturers. Overseas production may be unavoidable for some labor-intensive industries such as the textile industry. But it is probably more ideal for businesses that can easily transfer their service model overseas like restaurant franchises. Even for major corporations, overseas expansion involves taking high risks. Compliance issues and labor disputes, should they occur, may be troublesome and may shake the foundation of a small to mid-sized business.

Movements in exchange rates can also confuse business owners. When the exchange rate was one dollar to 80 yen there was a benefit for manufacturing products overseas and importing them to Japan. Four years later, when the yen was weak and depreciated further it was less appealing. Exports are becoming advantageous, but it is not easy to switch back and forth from domestic to overseas production. There are many cases of failure so it might be smarter to stay in domestic production even when it generates little profit.

In the case of our company, overseas production is not an option because I don't feel we would be able to find any better employees than those we employ here in Japan. They are tactful and have a good work ethic, good teamwork and a high potential to grow. Since our production process is complicated, overseas production is not suitable. And, there are no other countries than Japan where subway and bullet train systems run precisely to the minute.

Whatever your industry, be sure to investigate all the pros and cons and I believe that in most cases you will agree that overseas expansion is not the best option for the growth of your business.

Don't create unnecessary rules. German strategist Carl Philipp Gottlieb von Clausewitz stated that the harmful effect of a law-abiding principle is borne by adherence to formats. People like to make manuals for everything nowadays. In a service industry thorough manual correspondence is performed and repetitious checks for personal identifications is beyond the norm. I understand an ID check is necessary. But repetitive ID checks are performed beyond the norm only in Japan. What's your name? Are you Mr./Mrs. X? What is your birth date? What is the branch name of your bank? Is this protocol going to continue for the next twenty years?

The word "manipulating" has not been exported to Japan yet. But some rules do manipulate to a degree. For example, setting up a manual with rigid rules manipulates the individual's normal behavior. It takes away one's spirit and one's ability to be spontaneous, original and creative. I think even the ISO standard and compliance rules have had similar negative effects. Because of excessive compliances, bankers are complaining that the main duty in the financial industry is now creating documents. Germany is an advanced nation, famous for formalism. Yet it is meaningful that Clausewitz, who is a German strategist, pointed out the negative effects of such law-abiding principles.

I realize that some manuals and documents for compliance are required and that many businesses do not work out well without the ISO standards. However, I also believe that business leaders must transcend this growing law-abiding principle and conduct their businesses with a strong will and spirit. When they do this, their employees will be more motivated and creative. Also, I am very concerned that young people may work only under the guidance of a set of manuals. If they are too restrained by these rules, this may harm their potential and their futures.

CHAPTER 14

Five Fatal Flaws to Avoid

Acting too quickly. We live in the Internet age, which focuses on the speedy transfer of information. But acting quickly is not always the best thing to do. Previously, I mentioned how some companies quickly laid off employees in response to the Lehman Brothers' collapse. Because they acted so quickly they faced the challenge of not being able to start production when demand returned to the market. Had they waited patiently and observed the situations once demand returned to the market they likely would not have had to lay off their employees. When a drawn-out competition is expected it is rather foolish to act too quickly.

One of my favorite sayings quoted by the first Roman emperor is, "Festina Lente." This saying reportedly comes from the emperor while directing on the battlefield to "make haste slowly." In short, on a battlefield, depending on the situation, one may sometimes want to invade slowly and sometimes invade quickly, depending on all the factors. This is a philosophy that applies to business practices as well.

Unproductive meetings. Meetings rarely produce anything. Yes, the implementation of plans discussed in meetings occasionally lead to something positive. And, as stipulated by company law, board meetings and stockholders meetings do have specific goals and purposes. However, when a company has numerous meetings, overall they are usually not productive.

In many cases meetings are used to build consensus and confirm performance. Meetings and planning sessions are both time-consuming. Often meetings are held just to set up plans. Documents are created to hold meetings and then we also need to document the plans decided in the meetings. Good heavens, let me ask you—considering recent extreme geopolitical changes, do you think many of the plans made are executed as designed? The longer the term of the plans the more chances the plans will become insignificant. I wonder if Japan's leading electronics makers would have stayed in power as world leaders if their business plans had been executed as originally designed.

There are some exceptions. An exception might be the money and time spent to plan capital investments. In order to execute successfully any kind of capital investment preparations and meetings are needed. Additionally, as is the case with our company, a manufacturing company, we must hold staff meetings on our manufacturing process. While there are exceptions, our company never holds meaningless instructions or morning assemblies for empty greetings because these kinds of meetings are not productive activity.

It is a very dangerous idea when there is a tendency to believe that holding meetings is the same as completing tasks.

Not speaking up. Perhaps it is because I have a strong personality, but my relatives used to tell me that I needed to listen to others more carefully. Now, as I look back, I realize it is indeed important to listen to others carefully. However, one cannot survive in the world by just being honest and obedient. Many Japanese have silently listened to what elderly people said. Consequently, Japan's government debt is twice as much as its gross domestic product.

Of course it is very important to listen to others carefully. However, I think it is more important to have one's own opinion about the topics discussed. In Japan there is still a tendency that opinions are pushed just because they come from elderly people. But younger people need to hold fair and just attitudes and offer their own opinions as well.

Laying people off. Business leaders may be faced with situations where they have to lay off their employees. However, when employees who work in the production line are let go it can cause hard times later. It takes time to train production employees and if you let them go they will probably not come back. That means not only rehiring when production improves but it costs money while new employees have to be trained. Business leaders should keep their employees until the very last minute, even during times of little benefit or short-term deficits.

Major Japanese companies have been brainwashed by the lay-off and Return on Equity (ROE) management style that many U.S. companies practice. To align with stockholders' desires, companies may make a short-term profit by laying off their employees but this does not solve problems. Companies only struggle to make ends meet. Overall, this will provide a negative impact on the company's future and on the economy. It is a practice that U.S. companies need to re-evaluate as well.

Mass production. I believe that small to mid-sized companies should not focus on mass production because when demand changes, current machines may not be able to produce the product to meet the new demand. In this situation, small to mid-sized businesses, with little capital will face serious problems.

Ideally a small amount of products that can be used in multiple ways will eventually fulfill the goal of staying in business even if such a business model costs more. Just as in the case of televisions and solar panels, the mass production of such items is often shifted to low-cost countries and eventually the focus on such products loses competitiveness.

CHAPTER 15

Be Savvy About Finance

It is very rare to manage a business without debt. Therefore, business leaders must have as much knowledge as possible to manage their business. Financial affairs are very complicated nowadays. Many unusual actions occurred during the bubble economy. The abuse of subprime loans and credit default swaps are other examples of unusual actions that have happened.

As long as business leaders have a clear historical viewpoint and visions for their companies, the shortsighted thinking that financial institutions tend to fall into will not influence them. Financial institutions borrow money from the large banks with short-term interest rates. It is unavoidable for financial institutions to be influenced by government financial policy. Small to mid-sized manufacturing companies, however, share a different time concept from financial institutions. They view business in the long term, like ten to twenty years. While understanding this difference, business leaders need to build a good relationship with financial institutions. My philosophy for this is, "One must keep harmony but one doesn't necessarily have to agree."

Don't gamble. What I mean here is, don't gamble on an aggressive capital investment. Needless to say, it comes with high risk. Certainly it looks good to make a bold move and the media will often pick up on that. A flashy merger and acquisition (M&A) or a large-scale investment on which the fate of the company depends—there are many examples to mention of things that may not go well. In short, don't gamble if you are going to lose. A company may be rescued when it takes these kinds of risks if it is affiliated with a big corporation but for small to mid-sized companies, one mistake can end up being fatal.

Snap Decisions and Quick Action Needed in a Crisis. In a crisis, business cannot be done without snap decisions and quick actions. Some corporate leaders are happy as long as they can successfully fulfill their terms and collect their retirement benefits. The attitude is understandable in the large corporate system. However, this does not work with small to mid-sized business owners. They are fully responsible for the entire operations. When business is good, they can sit back. But when companies face a crisis, they must put their hearts and souls into their companies.

Intuition, speed and courage are necessary when a company is faced with a crisis. Business leaders must have the intuition to catch a hint of an upcoming big change and the ability to take appropriate measures and handle the change with speed and courage. All responsibilities are on their shoulders.

Personally, I remember the summer of 2008 when the Lehman Brothers' collapse occurred. I was on vacation in Singapore. I remember talking to my clients about a change in economic trends and also about the collapse of a U.S. subprime loan at a French bank. I felt something was wrong. As soon as I retuned to Japan I increased our cash holdings and paid attention to a move in the macro economy.

The sales of my company decreased by half in January 2009. I made an immediate decision to stop a plant operation for a few months. Stopping plant operations is critical in the manufacturing industry because a fixed cost is still booked. Our inventory unit price went up. Loss from inventory reevaluation was recorded and a huge amount of deficit was posted on the quarterly report in March 2009. However, by the summer of 2009 the economy had recovered and our sales made a V-shaped recovery. Ever since then our company has experienced revenue growth.

I often apply the 80-20 rule developed by Italian economist Vifredo Pareto. The Pareto principle states that for many events, roughly 80 percent of the effects come from 20 percent of the causes. For example, 80 percent of beer is consumed by 20 percent of heavy drinkers. In a project, 80 percent of the important work is completed during 20 percent of the productive period and the remaining 80 percent of the time is used to finish the remaining 20 percent of the work.

Business leaders are not artists, they do not need to make it perfect. What business leaders do need to do is to focus on 20 percent of the period when productivity is high.

In his book, *Essentialism: The Disciplined Pursuit of Less,* Gregg McKeown states that in order to succeed we should focus on only those things that are truly important and eliminate everything else. By understanding a theory of trade-off, business leaders can dramatically improve performance. If you look around you, you encounter variety television shows, Internet news, e-mails, cell phones, chats, SNS, games—all of which are distractions that eat up your time. McKeown stresses to now and then eliminate those noises and distractions. I cannot agree more. Perhaps it would do well to follow this philosophy: "Choose your distractions wisely because they will cost you dearly."

In times of crisis, leaders must make a quick decision on a countermeasure and run with it. With intuition, speed and courage I believe that I can overcome any crisis.

Cash helps out in a company crisis. Times have changed from being sales-oriented to being profit-oriented. However, no matter how large your profits are, they are not equal to your cash reserves. I'd like to focus on cash in case of emergency. For example, at the time of the Lehman Brothers' collapse things happened so quickly that financial institutions and companies became paranoid. Major restructuring occurred in multiple U.S. financial institutions. During that chaotic time, nobody cared about maintaining relationships or showing gratitude. All they could depend on was cash.

There is an English saying, "Cash is King." At the time of the Lehman collapse our company's sales declined by half. As a result, we recorded a negative balance in the 2009 fiscal year. It is likely fresh in everybody's memory that many major companies, including Toyota Motor Corporation, ran in the red at that time.

There was a time when we feared if we would be able to collect accounts receivable and it was quite difficult to borrow additional funds from financial institutions. Many companies showed a profit but did not have sufficient cash, thus consequently went bankrupt.

But times have changed. Companies need to hold on to considerable cash to continue their business. On a side note, please do not take this advice if you are reading this book ten or more years from 2016. This advice works only in current times when we have very low interest rates. I would give different advice if the interest rates were ten percent.

Manufacturing companies need to make capital investments such as in property and equipment. Therefore it is difficult to operate with cash only. In this case it is usually unavoidable to borrow funds from financial institutions. Here's what I learned from experience and common sense: A short-term loan, which must be paid back within a year, must ideally stay within the range of the amount where the total amount of accounts receivable and inventory is subtracted from accounts payable. Small to mid-sized companies are encouraged to utilize a long-term loan instead as it is easier to plan its repayment.

If a company leaves a huge amount of short-term loan unpaid the company faces a bad financial situation should things like the Lehman Brothers' collapse occur. Eventually the company will not be able to carry over the debt to the next account. In such a situation a financial institution will become desperate. This was the case with Lehman Brothers' and consequently it failed. Since the U. S. Federal Reserve Board became the last lender, the world economy managed to avoid bankruptcy.

As for profits, non-listed small to mid-sized companies should not get hung up too much on an indicator. It is rare that stockholders complain that the return on equity (ROE) ratio is low. The ROE ratio is a very useful indicator to estimate stock prices and evaluate mergers and acquisitions (M & A). In short, it shows how much profit each dollar of common stockholders' equity generates after subtracting debt from assets on the balance sheet, which is dissolution value. The ROE does not apply to small to mid-sized companies that do not frequently buy or sell stocks or businesses.

It is simplistic thinking and causes failure for small to mid-sized companies to follow the benchmark used by listed companies, ignoring the fact that business formats are different from that of listed companies. Major companies probably need policies for their dividends if they have public stockholders. In smaller companies, where owners are major stockholders, it is a silly measure to continue to pay high dividends unless there is a special reason. It causes excessive outflow of net worth after corporate taxation.

Since the continuation of business is key for small to mid-sized companies, they do not need to temporarily increase the ROE rate. I dare say the ROE is meaningless for small to mid-sized companies. When people take a bite of a piece of pizza, one bite might not particularly taste good while the entire pizza tastes delicious. The ROE examines whether that particular bite tastes good or not, it does not examine the pizza as a whole. Once the entire pizza is evaluated well it influences the entire balance sheet and positively impacts the return on assets (ROA). One piece of pizza does not a whole pizza make.

Listed companies talk a lot about the ROE and call it the ROE revolution, focusing on enhancing stock value. However, this is not relevant for small to mid-sized companies. The ROA is like the good taste of the pizza as a whole. It is important to focus on profits generated by the ROA and the balance sheet. A decrease in the figure of ROA means something is wrong. However, if a company strategically keeps a great deal of inventory the figure does decline.

In short, small to mid-sized business owners should not get caught up with indictors that have little to do with them.

Stakeholders consist of employees, business partners and stockholders, etc. A well-known business leader once said, "We must be clear that the company exists for stockholders." I disagree. I think that *everyone* involved in a business is a stakeholder.

Bottom line—keep calm and pick the right time. As I get older I have experienced many sufferings but they are not worth mentioning here. Instead I cite a quote by Akiko Takemura, an expert of I Ching: "You may face the time when nothing goes well no matter how hard you try. You may feel 'the time' is just like 'the winter of your life' where you feel that you cannot move forward. However, a problem is always solved and the spring always comes."

The seasons take turn naturally. However, when we humans are suffering we tend to lose calmness, we try to make changes. Despite the effort, it does not usually work in our favor. In life, there are many things that do not go as we wish. In order to make wishes come true we must catch the moment to address the problem and come up with a solution appropriate for the moment. I Ching teaches us to follow the law of nature so the problems are solved and our wishes come true.

As an example, no matter how hard you wish to harvest and plant seeds on the freezing ground during the winter season, there will be no harvest. However, when you plant seeds in the springtime the harvest will come. Only when our intentions coincide with the law of nature can things happen successfully.

It is true that some people may try to plant seed in the wintertime, hoping to overcome the sufferings as soon as possible. Unfortunately in this case, they will not see the harvest. I Ching teaches us that this is a shortcut and the best way to plant seeds is in the springtime when the right climate is there and the soil is nurtured. So it is with business so stay calm and pick the right time to make changes.

CHAPTER 16

A Few Final Thoughts

Don't Make Your Schedule Too Tight. Some people are constantly saying, "I'm busy." Of course people sometimes face situations that tend to make them feel busy. However, those who are constantly claiming how busy they are usually don't know how to effectively get their job done. To those people, acting busy is considered a virtue and they view it as if they are doing their jobs.

I have a fundamentally impatient personality therefore I have many experiences where I took action too quickly which resulted in mistakes and wasting time to fix the mistakes. Learning from these experiences I intentionally decided not to make my schedule too tight, leaving blanks in my day planner. The outcome is that I now have more room to breathe and am able to take the appropriate time for in-depth and strategic thinking.

Even when you don't purposefully schedule things, your planner will fill in as you do your work. When an urgent matter comes up you will be able to make room in your schedule to handle it. Imagine an example of a fire fighter, relaxing in a room but immediately jumping to action when the situation calls for it. You can take a chance or prevent a crisis by being able to respond to urgent matters by being flexible.

Strategic Stockpile. The Just-in-Time (JIT) inventory management system was once popular and many companies still employ it. JIT allows companies to minimize inventory in the supply chan. It's an efficient system in terms of production costs and avoiding excess inventory.

With the globalization of today's supply chain a major problem has arisen with JIT. It is very simple. Should unexpected events happen somewhere in the world the global supply chain can be cut off. Because JIT is designed to have no excess in inventory, when one point of the chain is stopped it results in no end product. This phenomenon actually happened all over Japan as well as other countries during the 2011 Tohoku earthquake and tsunami. Because Japanese companies were no longer able to manufacture their products, foreign companies experienced shortage in feedstock and parts. Due to JIT companies did not have stock in hand and were not able to manufacture their products.

Since our company had a plant in Fukushima Prefecture, we experienced a direct hit of the earthquake aftermath. Because of reputational damage, material delivery was stopped on the border of Ibaraki Prefecture. Literally, our lifeline was cut off. But, because I had a negative view about JIT as a result of the globalized supply chain, our company had stocked a few months worth of materials and products—some materials we had stocked a year's supply. Thanks to our inventory, our company sales right after the earthquake hit the highest record. Although we had to shut down the plant operation for a few months due to some damages we had enough stock so we did not face any major problems.

Don't be afraid to stockpile strategically.

Serendipity. Horace Walpole, a British politician and novelist, coined the word "serendipity" in the 18th century. Walpole was then staying on the island in Sri Lanka called "Serendip." In response to his encounter with a local fable, Walpole created the word "serendipity."

I have an impression that even many English-speaking people understand the definition of serendipity in a vague way. I am not speaking from an academic perspective however it is my understanding that the definition of "serendipity" is somehow similar to that of "synchronicity."

I think "serendipity" means an ability to catch the meaning of a coincidence and generate something from the coincidence. For example, it is a famous story that Alexander Fleming discovered lysozyme when he sneezed and also discovered penicillin when cleaning up his laboratory. These discoveries would not have happened without him constantly being problem-conscious.

There are more examples of such discoveries— Rubber tires by Goodyear Tire and Rubber Company, discoveries recognized by the Nobel Prize such as dynamite by Alfred Nobel, X-ray by Wilhelm Conrad Roentgen, radium by Marie Sklodowska-Curie and mass spectrometric analysis of biological macromolecules by Koichi Tanaka.

So pay attention to "serendipity" or intuition for your next big idea.

Make Foreign Friends. In order to exist and succeed in the world today you will need to globalize your relationships. Having friends and business partners overseas will bring you live information. By sharing issues with your friends and partners you will be more understanding about their positions. Understanding another's positions will help you when you negotiate.

Japan is currently facing various issues involving neighboring countries. I am not saying that we should be mystified by others but the analects of Confucius say, "Harmonize, but not agree." In short, it is important to be friendly, but that doesn't mean we have to always agree. Our company does many transactions with companies in China, South Korea and Taiwan. We have great partners in each country and exchange our opinions and information on a daily basis. In fact, this is helping us in conducting our business without any major issues. Because we deal directly with them, the information we obtain is speedy and precise.

One final Japanese philosophy. The Japanese Kanji symbol displays a stick in the middle, which means "to take a correct action suitable to a situation." The stick is symbolically in the middle, however the middle is not always the solution. A person who is not good at decision making often acts as if a problem can be solved by making a compromise such as combing parts of two different things into a new thing. But is a decision in the middle a true solution?

Let's say that there is one opinion that a company should develop a new product and another opinion that the company should not. Would it be a correct approach to invest only half of what is needed for the product development? The correct approach is to either develop the product or not.

Akiko Takemura, an I Ching expert, stressed the importance of taking a correct action suitable to a situation in I Ching. It is action-oriented, stressing the importance of taking a correct action suitable to a situation.

It is important for business leaders to take actions rather than to facilitate discussions. Moderation does not mean to take a popular, well-balanced action. It means to take the *correct* action suitable to the situation.

I hope sharing my beliefs and leadership philosophies in this book has provided for you some insights to consider as you make decisions that will help you as you continue to grow your business.

About the Author

Tomoaki Ota is president of Johoku Chemical Co. Ltd., Tokyo, a manufacturer of specialty chemicals for industrial applications, founded in 1958. Ota assumed the position of president at age thirty-six after the sudden death of his father in 2001. The global market share for some of the company's products exceeds 50 percent.

Since assuming the presidency, Ota has survived such crisis as the September 11 attacks, the Lehman Brothers' collapse, the Great East Japan Earthquake as well as the Fukushima nuclear disaster—all of which impacted the business. Despite these disasters, because of his unique business practices adopted from philosophy and history, Ota has led Johoku Chemical to double its sales, recording the highest sales and profits for six consecutive years.

Ota obtained a MBA from Southern Methodist University (SMU) in Dallas, and is a member of its

Cox School of Business Alumni Association Board. In 2012, 2013 and 2014 The Japan Times named Ota one of the 100 Next-Era CEOs in Asia.

Ota resides with his wife Mieko in Kamakura City, a suburb of Tokyo. They are the parents of two sons, Shin, who attends SMU in Dallas, Texas and Jo, who will attend Fountain Valley School of Colorado beginning the fall of 2016.

www.ingramcontent.com/pod-product-compliance
Lightning Source LLC
Chambersburg PA
CBHW030852180526
45163CB00004B/1543